"Thanks to my family and friends who supported me."

ISBN code: 9781704788111
Editorial Brand: Independently published

About the author -

 My name is Jean-Dominique PARIS and I live in the Paris region. After obtaining a baccalaureate, I continued my studies in work-study until I obtained an engineering degree from the C.N.A.M. (Conservatoire National des Arts et Métiers).

Diploma and experience that allowed me to join a large French group and to quickly reach positions of responsibility. At barely 30 years old -sorry for having understood too quickly how the French business system worked- and driven by a strong desire to help others, I decided to embark on entrepreneurship. Even as a child I sold to individuals, done the door-to-door, subscriptions to magazines made with an old computer and a small printer.

I have always wanted to bring my ideas to life.

Starting from a small company specializing in home computer troubleshooting for individuals, through real estate investments through a civil society, or through the development of mobile applications, I would like to share with you today my know-how on a subject **that is close to my heart and so important, personal and family budget education.**

Through this educational guide, the method I propose to you, I assure you, will make you financially richer from the very first months.

SOMMAIRE

WHO AM I? -

Why should you give me any credibility? Indeed, I have no diploma in this field and no financial management skills **or at least no knowledge outcomed of the school system.**

I am what is commonly called a self-taught person. I learned management, numbers, finance and financial independence through my education but also through my readings, training and all other types of materials.

My wife and I have two children aged 1 and 3 and each earn 2000€ net monthly income, which is less than the average salary in France, which is 2250€ net/month (Source: Insee and DADS, 2015 data published in 2017).
And yet... we own a house in the Paris region as well as two studios and finally we are shareholders in a real estate company with two properties for rent.

We eat quality food while favouring organic and local products.
Finally, we go on holiday every year and despite all this, we still manage to save hundreds of euros a month.

In addition, and it is important to note, we have not received **any inheritance or other money from the lottery.**

The objective is not to list our real estate and financial assets but to show you that properly managing your budget, accounts and money will allow you easily and without too much effort to achieve absolutely all your dreams on the sole condition that you kindly educate yourself financially

But what is financial education?

According to a definition of the O.C.D.E. Council (Organisation for Economic Co-operation and Development) of June 2005, financial education is the process by which consumers and/or investors:
1. Improve their knowledge of financial products, concepts and risks,

2. Acquire through objective information, instruction or advice, the skills and confidence necessary to:

    a. Become more sensitive to financial risks and opportunities,

b. Make informed, reasoned choices with full knowledge of the facts,

c. Know where to find financial assistance,

d. Take other effective initiatives to improve their financial well-being.

Or more simply, it means learning what money is, talking about it without taboos **and managing it correctly.**

On the government's website, there are figures for the least surprising or **even frightening**.

Indeed, when we know that money is omnipresent in our daily lives, in our society and in our world, it is unthinkable to read that "*85% of French people have not benefited from budgetary and financial education, whether at school, university, in their company or in a specialised institute* (Source: IFOP 2016 survey)".

You can imagine, that makes almost 9 out of 10 people who will, all their lives, use, spend, manage a budget, save, seek money when they have never been trained to do so.
Incredible, isn't it?

I invite you to do the test around you. In your family, among your friends, is money easy to talk about? Do you know your father's or your mother's salary? Who received financial education as part of their school curriculum? You will be surprised by the answers. This very important subject is not sufficiently taught.

In creating this guide, I wanted, modestly, to contribute to giving some keys to people wishing to understand the basic functioning of money, of a budget and allow everyone to make informed financial decisions.
This guide, I hope, will allow those who read and apply it to not only strengthen their financial stability but also to bring all their dreams to life.

Why the hell aren't they teaching financial education in school?

There are a lot of things that can justify why financial education is not taught in school:

1. *It would be detrimental to the wealthiest to introduce financial education courses into the current school system. Indeed, in the long term, the financial benefits of the richest may be eroded in favour of the emerging classes,*

2. *The threat of a recession,*

3. *The bankruptcy of the banking system,*

4. *And so on...*

I am not saying that the reasons mentioned above are not true, but as far as I am concerned, I simply think that the school is behind, very behind and has remained stuck in its 19th century functioning. Period of the agricultural era and then the beginning of the industrial era when it was good to "train" its workers and employees so that they obey their bosses blindly like good little soldiers and in order to be ever more productive.

But this era has changed and we live in a world where everything goes fast: **the information age.**

A world where you can become a millionaire in a snap of your fingers:

> ➢ *At 17, Nick D'Aloisio becomes a millionaire by selling an application to Yahoo,*

> ➢ *Kevin Systrom, the founder of Instagram, is only 25 years old when Facebook bought his application for a modest $715 million,*

> ➢ *By posting a video on YouTube, Justin Bieber becomes a millionaire,*

> *Etc…*

So although this guide doesn't cover this subject, **why not you?**

But be careful, I want to warn you, there are risks of getting rich overnight, especially if you have never received financial education. This may seem surprising to you, but how are you going to manage this money? To spend it, I'm sure you'll have many ideas, **but what about managing it**? You don't believe me? Yet this is what happened to many rich people who suddenly found themselves ruined:

Mike Tyson -

He found himself broke despite the $400 million he had raised during his boxing career. He spent his entire fortune in villas and cars before ending up with debts of over $50 million.

Chris Tucker –

You remember, he starred alongside Jackie Chan in the movies "Rush Hour". He pocketed over $50 million and lived in luxury before being caught up in his unpaid taxes and eventually found himself ruined.

Once again, the purpose of this guide is not to make you a millionaire, but what is true for these people is also true for those who have or will earn more money: a salary increases, an inheritance, a bonus, a lottery win, a pension, etc....

As soon as we earn even one extra euro we tend to spend it immediately so that our standard of living adapts to our new income; by operating in this way, you will never get richer, it is human, but the good news is that you can do something about it and that is precisely what I would like to work on with you.

By the end of this guide, it is certain that you will have made several hundred or even thousands of euros a year in financial resources. So I had to warn you and help you understand what money is, how to prepare for more money, how to manage it in a way that does not mean spending it anymore but spending it better but also making it grow.

WHY DID I WRITE THIS GUIDE?

All my childhood, I heard adults talk about money in all its forms: Dad's salary that you shouldn't disclose, the difficult end of the month that you shouldn't talk about, the taxes you have to pay and the criticism that comes from them, the debts you have to pay back and break up families, the home loans, the consumer loans, the expensive glasses you shouldn't break, the clothes you shouldn't damage and a whole bunch of other little sentences like that, which, I must admit, when I was a child had no meaning and no impact on me.
Why? Why? Simply because **no one had taken the time to explain to me** what money was and how it would fit into my or rather our daily lives.

And it is therefore by growing up, by becoming an adult that we understand the importance of money, the difficulty of earning it, of spending it, of preserving it but **above all of managing it.**

It took me several years to decipher, without pun intended, this very sensitive subject of money.

And one day, after hearing from colleagues, friends or family that they were overdraft all the time every month, that they were finding it harder and harder for them to make ends meet and that they couldn't have enough fun, I asked to a family member the following question: *"You say you don't have enough money, that it's hard for you to make ends meet, but do you know how much you miss it? Do you know how much you earn? Do you know how much is left for your "fun expenses" each month? »*.

At first, these innocently asked questions were hoping for rather simple answers such as: *"I am missing x hundreds of euros and I am currently earning x thousands of euros per month"*. But to my great surprise, the answer was not forthcoming to the point where I felt the discomfort on the other person's face.

He was desperate to answer me, but nothing, absolutely nothing, came out of his mouth. He thought over and over again and I concluded, very quickly, that this person, who often gave the impression of perfectly managing his money, was in fact only a "boaster" and could not even answer simple budget questions.

I was stunned! And that's the moment when I got a click. I wanted to help these people answer simple money questions and manage their budgets.

So, I created a tool for myself, which I have perfected over the years, that is very simplistic since it is none other than a fully automated spreadsheet:

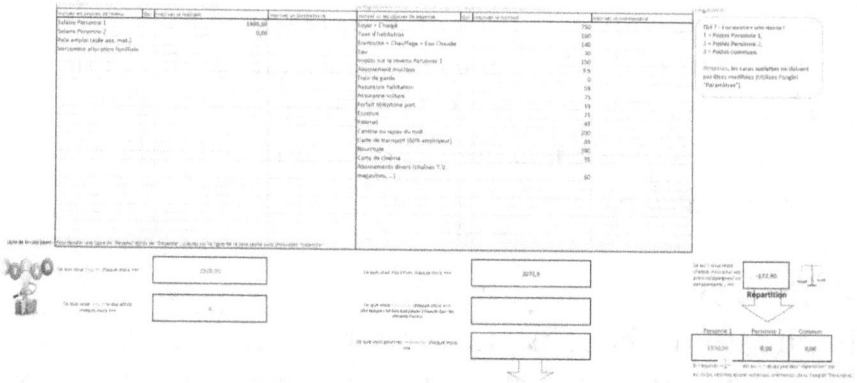

This spreadsheet will be useful to you throughout this reading and I invite you to download it from my website: **"https://jd-paris.fr/ressources/GERER_MES_COMPTES.XLSX"** (**N.B.**: please respect upper and lower case letters).

I then designed a very simple method around this tool that I personally tested before proposing it and then applying it to my whole family and even my friends.

This method I am talking about will be taught to you step by step throughout this practical guide. It details, with the greatest simplicity, the importance of money, the difficulty of earning it, of spending it, of preserving it but **above all of managing it**.

I invite you to follow this "recipe" to the letter and guarantee that you will not be disappointed. **All the people who applied it made money.**

Of course, it will never make you a millionaire, but you will be more serene about budgeting and your end of the month, that's for sure!

So please, go to the end of the method, don't start it without having the objective of finishing it.
Finally, be persistent and you will see the benefits very quickly.

And that... I guarantee it!

INTRODUCTION

➢ You pay various subscriptions to television channels (beIN SPORTS, Canal +, Canal Sat., O.C.S., SFR T.V.? Etc...), but how many do you really watch? Aren't there cheaper bouquets? Any other alternatives?

➢ You pay a movie card subscription, but how many times a month do you go there? Is it profitable? Wouldn't it be cheaper to take single seats? Have you already done the calculation?

➢ You pay tens or even hundreds of euros in car / home / credit insurance but also all kinds of packages, telephone / internet and this every month. And the comparators you know, do you use them?

➢ You tell yourself that you are making enough money: *"doing your accounts is not for me, I'm spending and we'll see. If I am in the red at worst, I would pay a few euros of agios"*, *"Look at my accounts? For what? I'm never in the red"*, *"I don't look at my accounts, it makes me anxious"*...
So? do you recognize yourself in these examples? I'm willing to bet yes, but don't worry, it's perfectly normal.

We all love these series of all kinds and this 50GB mobile package that allows us to watch more and more content.

Moreover, industrialists and banks know this very well and are getting richer as a result. **So let's stop enriching them or do it more consciously!**

If we take the example of banks, did you know that in 2018, the Banque de France had 46 billion euros in accounts receivable? Financial institutions are delighted because bank overdraft is an important source of revenue.

An irrefutable fact -

> *1 in 3 French people is exposed every month (take 3 friends or office colleagues around you, you can be sure that one is exposed this month),*

> *6 out of 10 French people experience an overdraft during the year.*

Let's get this over with!

Do you know how much you spend each month? How much money do you have left in your bank account for leisure and/or personal expenses? How much do you earn each month or how much could you save? How much do you have in case of hard times? Are your expenses really adapted to your needs? Etc.... Etc... Etc...

Go ahead! Go ahead! Please ask yourself these questions frankly. Really do it, stop reading for 5 minutes and ask yourself these questions.

So what about it? Did you know how to answer all the questions?

CHAPTER N° 1 - Do not suffer any more

"That's it, it's not the end of the month yet and yet I'm already the overdraft or at least it's just like",

"But why did I buy this thing, I'm never going to use it, it's stupid."

"It's much too expensive for me, it's a shame but I can't afford it,

"I would have liked so much to buy it from him, it would have made him so happy."

These stories may not be yours, but know that they are those of a large number of people living, some of them with the anguish of the end of the month, with the guilt of having spent money on things, which after the fact, seem useless to them or in the desire to reach, to access things that seem unaffordable to them.

Although I recognize that it is not always easy, I reassure you, nothing is lost since it is not inevitable either and you will, during this reading, understand, why and especially, how to obtain everything or almost everything you want.

Our world is full of places where temptations are strong. They are omnipresent and everything is done to make the desire to buy permanent. You will admit that it is so easy to let yourself be tempted, then take out your credit card and finally pay without even realizing it. Isn't that right?

Marketing is such that it does everything possible to trigger a maximum number of purchases from consumers that we are and, these sales techniques are present on e-commerce sites as well as in traditional stores.

Among those that are implemented to make you spend more and more, you will find:

The sense of urgency -

1. Indicate the stock level in real time for the product being consulted, this will create a sense of urgency that is all the more important when the stock level is low,

    Example on an online sales site -

    Il ne reste plus que 10 exemplaire(s) en stock (d'au

    Voulez-vous le faire livrer le samedi 21 oct ? Commandez-le dan

2. Indicate the number of times the item has been seen during the day to trigger more sales:

Examples for an online hotel room reservation site –

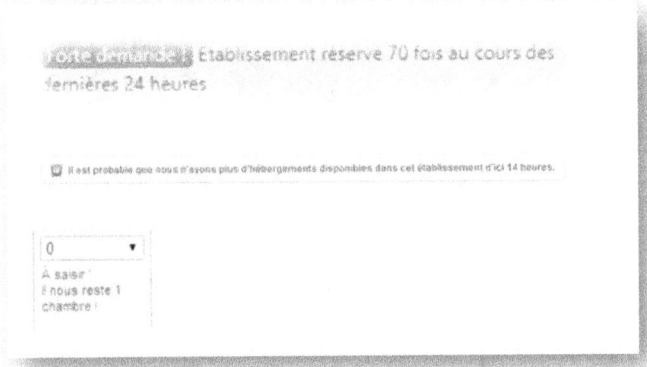

3. Flash selling is also a great way to get you to spend money quickly:

Example for an online product sales site –

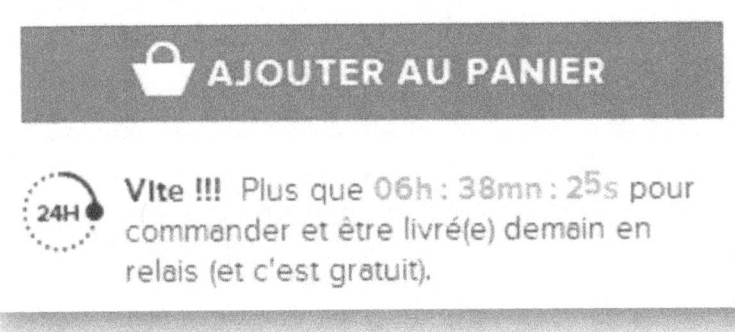

Confidence building -

The famous "satisfied or refunded". Simply displaying this information reassures your prospect (a prospect is a potential customer, he has not yet bought the product) and he does not feel trapped if the product does not ultimately interest him. And yet, did you know that legally you can return any product within 14 days? If so, it is very good because few people know it.

With this mention your prospect will buy a product more easily and, even if he does not like it, it is not certain that he will send it back.

Customer testimonials -

Before going any further and to be totally transparent with you, but also to avoid any criticism, it is a technique that I use myself on my website.

If you wish to view them, I invite you to go to: **https://jd-paris.fr/** under the heading **"THEY WITNESS"**.

Examples of customer testimonials on my website -

To come back to our subject, the most important e-commerce sites use it for almost everything, if not all their products, and if they do, it's because it works.

Customer feedback has become an essential part of marketing strategy.

As proof, in 2016, 85% of French people said they regularly used the Internet to find information before making a purchase and nearly 9 out of 10 Internet users consulted customer reviews to buy. Imagine the impact and influence this process can have on your sales or purchases.

Example on a very famous e-commerce site (amazon.fr) -

Commentaires client

⭐⭐⭐⭐⭐ 3

5,0 sur 5 étoiles ˅

5 étoiles	▓▓▓▓▓▓	100%
4 étoiles		0%
3 étoiles		0%
2 étoiles		0%
1 étoile		0%

Le plus cou

par Jean-Dominic

Format: Broché

Prix: 15,81 € + Li

Écrire un commentaire

And techniques of this kind exist by the thousands, whether in:

1. Product packaging. Everything is done to attract your attention and trigger your desire to buy,

2. The layout of the store and the departments (the favourite cakes, and often the most expensive, children are at their height, the cheapest brands are at the top or at the very bottom of the department...),

3. The psychological price: 19.90€ which seems **much** cheaper than 20€,

4. Sensory marketing. Be honest, who has never missed a bakery that smelled like chocolate bread and didn't think, *"Here, I'll buy one for myself.*

The result is irrefutable, you buy more, sales and profits explode for the benefit of stores and you end up, in the best of cases, with objects that are useless to you or worse with a bank account in the red.

It never happened to you after you bought an item to say to yourself: *"but why did I buy that? What the hell am I supposed to do with it? "*.

I remember a friend who left for a wedding in Italy, who wanted to go shopping at all costs for the simple and only reason that she had heard that in Italy the prices were cheaper.
As she contemplated the handbags through the windows, she began to enter and buy one. A few minutes later, she came out with no less than fifteen handbags.
When I asked her why she had bought so many, she replied that they were really cheap and that it was a great opportunity.
It was only much later that she realized that she had bought too much.

She then said to me: "*But what am I going to do with all this, I'm sure I'll never use it, do you think I'll be able to return them? »*.

Please! Please! Stop being subjected to all these external influences and **regain control!**

To help you in this process, I propose below a list of things for which I think you should no longer spend money:

Bank fees - There are comparators that, depending on your profile, tell you which banks to go to and how much you will **actually** save.

Be careful, not all comparators are good to follow. Personally, the one I use is excellent in the sense that it is guaranteed 100% neutral. Unlike the vast majority of banking comparators in the market, this one is not remunerated by banks.

The purpose of this 100% neutral comparator is to present the bank rates of most institutions, and to allow consumers to orient themselves according to their needs.

The tool has no link of any kind whatsoever, nor direct or indirect interest, with the referenced professionals. I insist, he receives no remuneration from the referenced professionals and that is what makes all the difference.

All banks on the site are treated with absolute fairness.
All you have to do is enter a place of residence, your current bank, the package subscribed and the bank card used.

The Internet user then accesses the list of banks corresponding to the profile entered, classified in ascending order of annual pricing.
For each bank, the annual cost, the achievable savings and the details of the fees are detailed.
Come on, I'm not making you simmer any longer, I'm obviously talking about the UFC comparator Que-Choisir that you can find by following the link opposite: **https://www.quechoisir.org/,** section ::

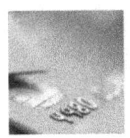

Comparateur banques • Comparez les tarifs bancaires

Extended warranty - Whether it's for a tumble dryer, MP3 player, steam generator, high-definition TV or any other electronic device, sellers systematically urge you to subscribe to the famous 5-year extended warranty. It is expensive, only increases the seller's commission, empties your wallet and all for what? **For nothing...**

Did you say for nothing? And yes, according to a very serious study carried out by the association 60 million consumers: *"warranty extensions are often useless because, contrary to the arguments put forward by the sales representatives, the devices are not less and less reliable. The failure rate of the devices is only 2% in the first year, mainly due to manufacturing defects, and these repairs are fully covered by the manufacturers' warranties. After the first year, less than 1% of the devices fail due to manufacturing defects. Problems related to wear and tear only appear after five years, the longest period of warranty extensions.* **And it is for these reasons that this extension of the guarantee is totally unnecessary.**

Gambling games - The chances of winning the lottery are almost nil, I spare you the undrinkable formula that calculates your probability of winning but this one is thin...

Let's take an example: To win the lottery, you have to choose 5 good numbers from a grid that has 49 numbers, so there are no less than 2 million (1,906,884 to be exact) different ways to complete the grid. You also have to find the lucky number. And in the end you will have 1 chance in nearly 20 million (19,068,840 to be exact) to win the jackpot, a probability of **0.000005244 %.**

Wouldn't it be more fruitful to use this money to build up savings or invest it in something that pays you back?

Various and varied subscriptions - We will see this in a next chapter, but do you really use your subscriptions? Are they really adapted to your needs? If the answer is no, then why not sort it out?

In this guide, we will help you step by step and in the simplest possible way to better manage your budget and save money. If you apply this method to the letter, you will benefit from it from the first month.

It is not a miracle recipe that we will present to you, but a series of simple actions and reflexes to have that will make you financially richer.

The method will guide you through concrete examples, which are not useful to implement at once. You can perfectly start applying some principles, stop and then come back to them a few days later.

The objective is to make you gradually assimilate the advice and information given so that it becomes natural for you to use and apply them in your daily life.

This is not about "head stuffing". On the contrary, learn at your own pace, take your time. Moreover, you will see for yourself that this method is simple and makes a lot of sense.
Indeed, it is not necessary to have completed a +5 baccalaureate to understand and apply it, you just have to follow the guide and progress at your own pace, nothing more.

Did you say common sense? What's the point of teaching me then?
Simply because this method is so easy that no one thinks of implementing it, and yet it requires very little effort and will greatly improve your comfort and **above all your finances**.

See below some examples of things that are so simple to implement but that no one applies and that could greatly improve your daily life:

1. Playing sports 7 minutes a day, *rather than watching television*, is excellent for your health, increases life expectancy and reduces the risk of disease. And yet, still too few people apply it and prefer to find good excuses not to do so. I invite you to test "7 minutes workout" every day for 30 days and you will be won over. It's 100% at home, 100% without equipment and 100% free,

2. Meditation increases your concentration, reduces the risk of anxiety, improves your memory capacity, promotes better sleep and takes only 10 minutes a day. So why not test it? I recommend the "Petit Bambou" application to introduce you to it,

3 Learning a language will only take you 10 minutes a day with applications like Mosa-Lingua or Duolingo. The method used is much more proven and effective than that of the school system. Get started!

4. How much time do you spend in traffic jams or public transport? *"According to a Euro Car Parts study, it takes the French an average of 3.5 hours to get to work every week, preferably by car"*. And why not use this time to learn a language, listen to audiobooks or simply learn, cultivate...

This method was created to meet the expectations of as many people as possible. Whether you are a mechanic, plumber, lawyer, engineer, store clerk, secretary, nurse, worker or even doctor, this method is for you. If you apply it, you will get richer.

*"Most people look at things as they are and wonder why? I look at things as they might be and ask Why not? "***J.F Kennedy**

So now it's your turn to play!

SUMMARY -

✓ Don't let yourself be influenced by sales and marketing techniques of any kind,

✓ Compare the offers with 100% neutral tools,

✓ Ask yourself the right questions: Do I really need it? Is it adapted to my needs? And so on...

✓ Apply this method at your own pace, do not be in a hurry to finish it, the objective is to gradually assimilate the practical advice so that it becomes a reflex.

And above all, be free:-)

CHAPTER 2 - Financial Stability

Do you know these little sentences: *"I'm just enjoying a point, that's all! Money is made to be spent, right? We're not gonna bury you with your money as far as I know! »*.

Perhaps you yourself have used them... Having fun is great and **doing it while controlling your budget is even better**.

Every month and year millions of French people are exposed:

> ➤ *1 in 3 French people is exposed every month,*

> ➤ *6 out of 10 French people experience an overdraft during the year,*

> ➤ *At the end of 2015, 843,000 households were over-indebted, or 1.5 million people,*

> ➤ *At the end of 2015, 2.7 million people were registered in the National Register of Incidents for the Repayment of Credits to Individuals.*

And to think that these figures could drastically decrease :-(

And if you knew exactly how much tax you still have to pay, how much you have left at the end of each month and how much you can spend or save for your personal pleasure, wouldn't that be better? Wouldn't you approach the end of the month in a more serene way?

Of course, I'm not talking about making sophisticated calculations that will take up all your time, but rather about using a very simplistic tool that you will have completed once and for all in a few minutes and that can give you an overview of your financial situation at a glance. **So, are you ready?**

In the rest of this reading, you will learn and then understand how to achieve financial stability and get rid of the anxiety and even fear of the end of the month.

Financial stability is not only about having positive accounts and/or being in the "green" at the end of the month, it is also about being able to look to the future with confidence, have plans and be able to make them happen

I can reassure you, nothing very complicated. To achieve financial stability, you have to take the shortest path, and yes, you read it well, the shortest path that for once is not full of pitfalls and all the other obstacles that could slow you down and put you off.

You will simply need to have a detailed knowledge of all your expenses and income, period! It will require almost no effort on your part. I say "almost" because the only efforts you need to make are common sense and will very quickly become habits and then reflexes. Pretty cool, right?

I see you coming, when I say "make an effort", it is obviously not a question of stopping enjoying yourself, quite the contrary, but rather of continuing to do so with greater serenity. Enough talk, let's get to the heart of the matter

SUMMARY -

✓ Too many people are out in the open every month, and if you could avoid it,

✓ It is important to know what you earn to know what you can spend. Is this your case?

✓ Knowing your budget will allow you to better manage your expenses and achieve financial stability,

✓ There is no question of stopping enjoying yourself. On the contrary, you will be able to combine pleasure and serenity.

CHAPTER N° 3 - Expenditure

"The most important thing is not the money but the way it is spent. " (Abyssinian Chronicles - Moses Isegawa)

Indeed, who is the richest? The one who earns 1,500€ and spends 1,000€ or the one who earns 20,000€ and spends 25,000€...

The Larousse definition and its example clearly reflect reality: *"Action to spend money, to use it: To make reckless expenditures"*.

And the synonyms are just as sad: *fresh, ruined, wasted, squandered, slammed, etc.*

However, spending money is not an evil in itself. As a friend of mine often told me: *"Spend your money while there is still time, we won't bury you with it"*, and that said she was absolutely right. Nevertheless, it is advisable to spend it "intelligently". Although everyone has their own way of looking at things, there are expenses that can be avoided or reduced.

In this exercise, you will learn how easy it is to take stock of what you spend each month. The exercise will only take you 30 minutes and once and for all.

Case study - Review of my expenses

The following exercise is an example and should of course be adapted to your personal situation.

Just follow the two steps below to find out your monthly expenses. You can stop at any time between steps.

Are you ready to go? It's up to you!

Step N°1 -

➤ Retrieve your last 3 current account statements:

Relevés papier -

Relevés en ligne -

☐ MAI 2018 ☐ télécharger

☐ JUIN 2018 ☐ télécharger

☐ JUILLET 2018 ☐ télécharger

➤ Identify recurring samples (which come back every month) and highlight them in yellow, for example:

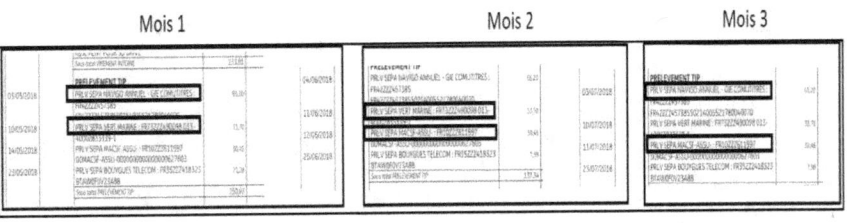

Step 2 -

> Open the account management tool found at the following address: " **https://jd-paris.fr/ressources/GERER_MES_COMPTES.XLSX** " (N.B: case sensitive) and fill in thecolumn "Expenses" as follows:

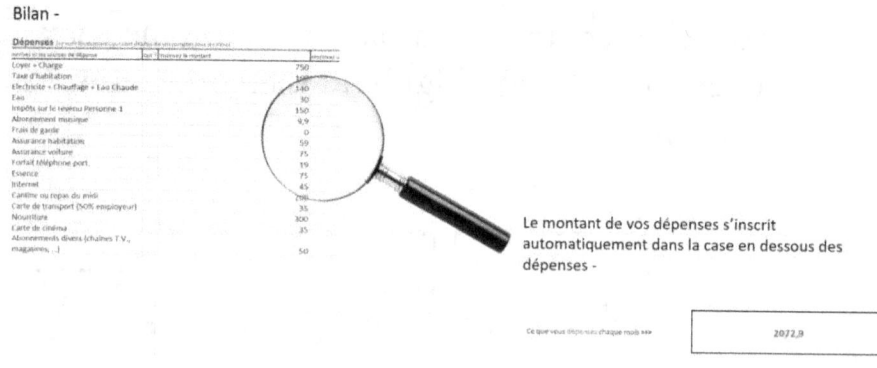

Dépenses (ce sont les montants qui sont débités de vos comptes tous les mois)

inscrivez ici les sources de dépense	Qui ?	Inscrivez le montant		Inscrivez u
Loyer + Charge			750	
Taxe d'habitation			100	
Electricité + Chauffage + Eau Chaude			140	
Eau			30	
Impôts sur le revenu Personne 1			150	
Abonnement musique			9,9	
Frais de garde			0	
Assurance habitation			59	
Assurance voiture			75	
Forfait téléphone port.			19	
Essence			75	
Internet			45	
Cantine ou repas du midi			200	
Carte de transport (50% employeur)			35	
Nourriture			300	
Carte de cinéma			35	
Abonnements divers (chaînes T.V., magasines, ...)			50	

Postes de dépenses principaux des Français

Inscrivez ici le montant qui vous est débité chaque mois

Inscrivez vos postes de dépenses et les montants que vous avez relevés précédemment :

N.B. - The expense items presented in the tool are examples, you can of course add and/or delete them.

Résultat -

Bilan -

Dépenses

Loyer + Charge	750
Taxe d'habitation	100
Electricité + Chauffage + Eau Chaude	140
Eau	30
Impôts sur le revenu Personne 1	150
Abonnement musique	9,9
Frais de garde	0
Assurance habitation	59
Assurance voiture	75
Forfait téléphone port.	19
Essence	75
Internet	45
Cantine ou repas du midi	200
Carte de transport (50% employeur)	35
Nourriture	300
Carte de cinéma	35
Abonnements divers (chaînes T.V., magasines, ...)	50

Le montant de vos dépenses s'inscrit automatiquement dans la case en dessous des dépenses -

Ce que vous dépensez chaque mois →

2072,9

In summary -

1.   Take back your last 3 current account statements,

2.   Identify recurring samples (which come back every month) and highlight them in the color of your choice,

3.   Fill in the columns in the account management tool by adding :

   a. Expense items (by default, the items are already filled in, you can add additional items),

   b. The amount for each expense.

   ➢ This will give you the amount spent each month.

At this stage it is possible that you do not yet see the benefits and yet it is already a hell of a job done.

To make sure you haven't missed a thing and to definitively close this chapter, I propose a little quizz/advice:

1.As time goes by and my desires change, my family situation can also change. So what should I do to make sure I always know what I'm spending?

Solution: Resume step 1 with my last updated account statements.

2.I have unsubscribed from my gym, what should I do immediately?

Solution: Delete the line in the expense screen presented in step 2. You just saved 30€, well done!

Well done, you finished the expense part, easy, didn't you? And the rest is just as simple.
Don't give up anything!

SUMMARY -

> ➢ Remember that the most important thing is not the money but the way it is spent (Abyssinian Chronicles - Moses Isegawa),

> ➢ You can have a salary of 20,000€ per month, if your expenses are higher, you will still be poorer than a person who earns 1,500€ per month and has only 1,000€ of expenses,

> ➢ It is important to know what you are spending every month,

> ➢ Have a small document that records your expenses,

> ➢ Don't have a complicated document to follow on a daily basis, start with something simple that groups your most important positions and review it every 3 months.

CHAPTER N° 4 - Income

As in the previous chapter, let us start with the definition of Larousse.

Income - *"What is received, in kind or in money, by someone or a community as the result of invested capital (interest on loaned capital, dividend on committed capital), or as remuneration for an activity (profit) or work (salary).*
"

This time, the synonyms are enticing: *gain, annuity, remuneration, dividends, etc.*

The income, for the vast majority of individuals, is the result of their work. But like many, you can never have enough. If you're normal? Of course, it is human nature to want more and more. Let's take an example: You earn 1300€ net per month, you live in a small studio in the Paris suburbs and have a rather simple life.

You do your shopping, pay your rent and your bills (telephone, internet, TV, etc.); from time to time when you have the opportunity to work overtime, you do it willingly and you think that it will improve your comfort and allow you to enjoy extras such as a restaurant with friends, buying new clothes and/or shoes or just doing or enjoying yourself. Then one evening you get together for a drink with your friends and the famous discussion comes up: *And if only I could earn a few more euros...*

That's it, you're dreaming of even 1600€ net per month, after all, what's 300 euros more for your boss? And imagine how it could change your life forever. You're certain of it, you need the money. But then how do you get it? Change jobs? Not too constraining and then you're fine where you are. Have a little job next door? Too tiring and you have to keep time for yourself, after all life is not only work but also leisure. Request a raise? Well why not... The next morning you go to your boss, discuss and finally he accepts *(I grant you it's never that simple, but you'll quickly understand where I'm going with it)*

That's it, you are at the head of a higher income, 1600€ net per month, and you say to yourself that the studio is starting to be small and then you would like your sweetheart to move in with you. You go to classified ads sites and quickly find a larger accomodation for a few hundred euros more per month. In addition, you are tired of pasta every night and cans and decide to take other more expensive but oh so much better products, after all it is only a few tens of euros more in total and then you have had an increase so you can afford it. You also do more outings with friends and one evening, a few months later, you find yourself in the same bar where you were discussing salary. And to your great surprise and despite this extra 300€ per month you are again close to red and would like to earn even a few more euros.

So how did you get into this? Is the spell on you? Of course not, you do like most people, you adapt your standard of living to your salary, so you can never get enough. Your situation changes (child(ren), marriage, P.A.C.S), your desires too (new job requiring a tailor, suit...). You constantly adapt your situation to changes in your income.

But then how do we get out of this vicious circle? Will you stay in this spiral forever? Does that mean that there is no point in wanting more because we will never be satisfied anyway?

Don't panic, of course not, once again it's quite normal to want more and to adapt your standard of living as a result of your increased income. I invite you to continue reading and **I guarantee that at the end of this book you will be able to transform this vicious circle into a virtuous one.**

There is nothing better than a practical exercise to illustrate the control of your income.

Case study - Review of my income

As in the previous case study, simply follow the steps below to find out in detail your monthly income. And don't forget, the main thing is to complete this method, so you can stop at any time between steps.

Are you ready to go? It's up to you!

Step N°1 -

> ➤ Retrieve your last 3 current account statements:

Relevés papier -

Relevés en ligne -

- ☐ MAI 2018 ⬇ télécharger
- ☐ JUIN 2018 ⬇ télécharger
- ☐ JUILLET 2018 ⬇ télécharger

> ➤ Look for recurring transfers (marked SEPA) (which come back every month) and highlight them in green, for example:

Mois 1   Mois 2   Mois 3

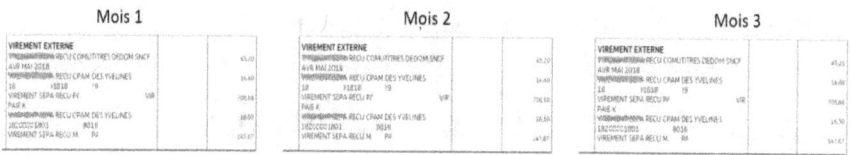

Step 2 -

> ➤ Open the account management tool and fill in the "Settings" tab as follows:

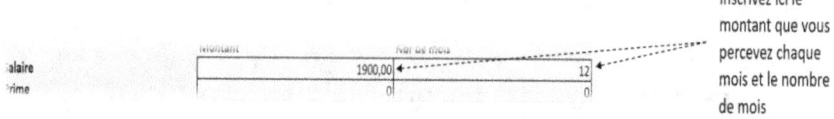

Inscrivez ici le montant que vous percevez chaque mois et le nombre de mois

Step 3 –

Inscrivez ici les sources de revenus et montants que vous percevez chaque mois HORS SALAIRE (si vous ne percevez aucune aide de l'état, aucun autre revenu que votre salaire >>> Ne rien n'inscrire)

Résult –

Le montant de vos revenus s'inscrivent automatiquement dans la case en dessous des revenus -

In summary -

- ✓ Take back your last 3 current account statements,

- ✓ Identify recurring transfers (which occur monthly) and highlight them in the colour of your choice,

✓ Fill in the columns in the account management tool by adding :

a. The amount of salary income,
b. Other income (OTHER THAN WAGES) and the amount of each of these income.

➢ This gives you the amount received each month.

Well done, you finished the income part.

At this stage of reading, there are two types of people, those who say to themselves: "*It's true that it's very simple, why I didn't do it before... Finally, I start to see things more clearly.* " and those who say: "*Great, all this I already knew, well I didn't apply it, but what interests me is the famous 13th month that the title of this guide promises me* " **>>> Don't worry, we're getting there.**

In the next chapter we will discuss the importance of a good balance between income and expenditure.

SUMMARY -

✓ It is the human being's characteristic to always want more, so you are normal:-),

✓ Do you know how much you earn each month? Payroll, various payments, etc...

✓ Your needs change, constantly evolving over the course of your life. Adjusting your standard of living to a recent increase, promotion, bonus, etc... is normal, but don't fall into a vicious circle, prefer a virtuous circle.

CHAPTER N° 5 - An imperfect balance

In previous exercises, you may have noticed that I use an example to guide you.

This example shows the situation of a person with no dependent children and earning a salary of about €22,000 net per year (median salary in France in 2018), or about €1,900 net per month. You must obviously adapt it to your personal situation (dependent child (s), spouse (s)...), everything is done to ensure that the practical exercise fits your situation as closely as possible.

But let us return to what interests us and to one of the most important parts: **balance**.

What is balance? Be careful this definition may change your life forever, are you ready? Are you comfortable sitting down?

So here we go! Balance is the difference between your income and your expenses. Wow, impressive, isn't it? And as simple as it may seem, very few people do this exercise, which is so easy to implement. Once you know the balance between your cash inflows and outflows, it is very easy to determine how much you need to raise to rebalance your bank account.

So you know what you have left or what you lack each month for your personal pleasures, your savings, your hardships, Christmas gifts, etc... etc...

In our example, you would have to reduce your expenses by 172.90€ per month:

1900 €

2072,9 €

=   - 172,9 €

Chaque mois vous dépensez plus que ce que vous gagnez il faut donc rééquilibrer vos comptes

Revenus   Dépenses

Remember, in the previous exercise you said you earned 1900€ net per month and spent 2072,90€ per month. The difference is therefore 1900€ - 2072,90€ or a lack of 172,90€ each month.

Does the challenge seem impossible to you? It is very simple and accessible to anyone. I invite you to read the next chapter without further delay, which will certainly lead you to financial stability and your 13th month.

Are you skeptical? It's normal, I have
I myself was surprised by all the savings I was able to achieve and made my family and friends realize through this implementation that I call the A.B.C. of savings.

SUMMARY -

✓ Do you know the difference between your income and your expenses?

✓ Balance is essential in the management of your budget:

= -172,9 €

Chaque mois vous dépensez plus que ce que vous gagnez il faut donc rééquilibrer vos comptes

Revenus   Dépenses

✓ Always be balanced and you will be richer.

CHAPTER N° 6 - The A.B.C. of economies

Every time you make a purchase, an expense or consult your bank statement, it is advisable or even important to ask yourself certain questions.

Be careful, far be it from me to blame you for spending, but sometimes just wondering if it's really useful can save you a lot of money and make you regret it.

Come on, think about it, haven't you ever made a purchase that you regretted immediately after you went to the checkout? Personally, this has happened to me several times. I remember one day, when we were walking around in a high-tech store, passing by a game console, the Wii U. Although we both knew it was a very bad idea, we looked at each other with my wife and were both excited about spending several sleepless nights playing Mario Kart. Immediately said, immediately done, we bought the console and everything that goes with it. After the euphoria of the first few days and after playing it for only a few hours, we thought to ourselves: "*why did we buy this console...*" and so we sold it almost half as expensive as what we had paid for it.

At least it had the merit of making a little boy happy, you can imagine, a brand new console at half price and still under warranty. The mother who came to buy it for me couldn't believe it, she even thought it was a scam. Well, not at all, the only ones who were harmed in this story were us.

To limit the desire and avoid any regret, I suggest that you apply the following method whenever you wish to make an expense.

A - Is it **S**uitable for my needs?

Your needs today are changing and are certainly different from those you had a few years or even months ago.

There are several possible causes: new job, separation, loss of financial resources, children, home, new passions...

The simple fact of asking yourself this question: "Is it really adapted to my needs? ", may be enough to buy something more suitable, sometimes cheaper or simply not to buy anything.

We will see more concrete examples below.

B - Do I really Need it?

According to the Elabe Institute, 40% of consumers in France have subscribed to more than six subscriptions, or nearly one in two French people, and 7% more than eleven.
The average number of subscriptions per French consumer increased significantly, from 3.2 in 2012 to 5.4 in 2016 (Source: CSA Institute).

Today, French consumers are active on average on 5.4 subscriptions.

But are they really useful?

Let's take the example of sports halls: More than 6 out of 10 people stopped going there within the first 6 months after their registration (Source U.F.C. Que-Choisir). And of course continued to pay... A godsend for sports halls.

Finally, there are many ways or means of comparing today, do you do that?

C - Have I Compared the offers?

Since 1 January 2015, the Hamon law allows you to change your insurance at any time, after one year of commitment. Did you know that?

Certainly, but most people don't, simply because we all have a busy life, with a job, children to manage, etc... etc... etc...

But have you ever taken the time to think about all the savings you could make by looking at this subject for even a short hour?

Come on, let's do the math! How much do you earn on average?

Let's take 2250€ net per month which is, I remind you, the average salary in France in 2018 (Source: Insee and DADS, 2015 data published in 2017). You work an average of 21 days a month and about 7 hours a day (35 hours a week).

The calculation is simple: The number of hours worked for a month is: 21 days x 7 hours / days = 147 hours.
Your hourly rate is therefore about: 2250€ / 147 hours = 15,31€ for one hour of work.

What does all this mean? What am I getting at?

Quite simply that to make the hour I mentioned above profitable, which will allow you to save money, you will have to find 15.31€ in your drawer funds. This small amount or rather this time spent can bring you hundreds, even thousands of euros a year.

Does that seem insurmountable to you? Don't you think it's worth it?

Let us see in our concrete example what could respond to the A.B.C. of economies:

Dépenses (ce sont les montants qui sont débités de vos comptes tous les mois)

Incrivez ici les sources de dépense	Qui ?	Inscrivez le montant		Inscrivez u
Loyer + Charge			750	A
Taxe d'habitation			100	
Electricité + Chauffage + Eau Chaude			140	A,C
Eau			30	
Impôts sur le revenu Personne 1			150	
Abonnement musique			9,9	B
Frais de garde			0	
Assurance habitation			59	C
Assurance voiture			75	C
Forfait téléphone port.			19	A,C
Essence			75	
Internet			45	A,C
Cantine ou repas du midi			200	A
Carte de transport (50% employeur)			35	
Nourriture			300	A
Carte de cinéma			35	B
Abonnements divers (chaînes T.V., magasines...) magasines, ...)			50	B

Legend -

A - Is it **S**uitable for my needs?
B - Do I really **N**eed it?
C - Have I **C**ompared the offers?

Remember to adapt this example to your personal situation. Go ahead, really do it, pause your reading and apply the method.

Example N°1 -

Is your rent adapted to your needs? I grant you this item of expenses is complicated to modify quickly but it must nevertheless be studied.

Indeed, if your children have left home and you are still paying rent for a 3-bedroom apartment, it might be a good idea to think about it, right?

Example N°2 -

Are all subscriptions (cinema, music, magazines, television channels...) adapted to your needs? Do you use them to the point of paying for a subscription?

Personally, I like to go to the cinema from time to time and seeing the price of the tickets, between 9€ and 13€ per person, I had undertaken with my partner to subscribe to the unlimited cinema card. Two years and 840€ later (at my time the unlimited duo version was at 35€/month, which remains pretty much the same today) I realized that this offer was not at all adapted to my needs.

Indeed, I went there twice a month at the beginning then very quickly once a month then no more the first year at all. The second year has arrived, so have the new resolutions and we promised to go 2 or 3 times a month. And finally, we followed the same pattern as the previous year....

So if we had taken out of subscription places, we would have paid: ~ 396€ for both years instead of €840, i.e. an in two years and a monthly saving of 3718.5€.

Example N°3 -

There are hundreds of ways to compare offers; the best and most effective way is through online comparators. There are many of them and for all types of needs (car insurance, home insurance, banking, phone plan, internet subscription...).

For my part, I have a preference for the comparators presented on the U.F.C. website Que-Choisir (https://www.quechoisir.org/). Admittedly, you have to pay an (per month) to access it, but it is guaranteed to be 100% neutral.
Believe me, it's really worth it. You will have access to hundreds of comparators, guides and product tests of all kinds. You're not getting screwed anymore!

Well, you're going to tell me, it's great all these examples but in practice what does it give?
I invite you to read the next chapter to get to the heart of the matter and make your first concrete savings.

SUMMARY –

✓ Don't regret a single purchase, a single expense,

✓ Ask yourself the right questions:

1. Is it **A**dapted to my needs? **No**, then change,

2 . Do I really **N**eed it? No then sell it, terminate it, etc....

3.Have I **C**ompared the offers? **No**, then do it: -)

Chapter 7 - Immediate savings

There are different ways to save money. In this chapter, we will learn a direct and very easy to implement one that will require little or no effort.

First of all, the immediate savings...... Most of the time it's those savings for which we say: "*Oh yes, I should unsubscribe, I haven't used it for a long time*" or "*I didn't even know I was paying for it anymore, I really need to cancel my subscription*". And then, immediately said immediately forgotten, or we don't really know how to do it, to whom to send the mail, a registered letter or a simple letter, what to stipulate in the mail, what to provide as a document, etc..., etc....

All these things make it possible to constantly postpone these actions until the next day, while not only are there free ways to get help: **Google is your friend**, just type in the search engine: "*Letter of termination of my xy subscription*" to find hundreds of examples of free letters:

Lettre de résiliation abonnement internet : M

https://www.merci-facteur.com › Modèles de lettres d

★★★★★ Note : 4,5 - 18 327 votes

Rédigez rapidement votre **Lettre de résiliation abonnement**
générales d'**abonnement**, **résilier mon abonnement intern**

Recherches associées

lettre de résiliation internet sfr

lettre résiliation internet déménagement

lettre résiliation internet free

lettre de résiliation

lettre de résiliation

lettre de résiliation

[PDF] Modèle de lettre de résiliation - Boutique

https://boutique.orange.fr/medias/pdf/divers/pdf-lettre-typ

Objet : **résiliation de mon abonnement** à votre service d'ac
société un contrat d'**abonnement** concernant l'accès au serv

Résiliation abonnement internet - Modèles d

www.modele-lettre-type.com › Lettre résiliation., annulatic

Or turn to free services such as public writers at the
C.C.A.S. (Centre Communal d'Action Sociale) in your
city. Ask your Town Hall for more information.
Also remember that some subscriptions do not even
require a letter, a simple click on : *"cancel my
subscription"* is enough.

Example for the very famous subscription video on demand site –

Or Audible, AmazonPrime, Free phone package, B and You....

>>> With a simple click your subscription will be cancelled the following month.

Otherwise, be sure that a registered letter with acknowledgement of receipt will be sufficient to cancel a subscription to the service in question (address that you can easily find on the Internet). And even for those who do not want to go to the post office to send this letter, it is possible to write it and send it directly from the post office website:

Lettre Recommandée en ligne - Boutique Particuliers La Poste
https://boutique.laposte.fr/lettre-recommandee-en-ligne ▼
Lettre recommandée en ligne. 1. Déposez votre document. 2. Saisissez les coordonnées de votre (vos) destinataire(s). 3. Payez en ligne sur un site securisé. 4.

Let's now look at what is eligible for immediate savings.

Let's take up our practical case –

Dépenses (ce sont les montants qui sont débités de vos comptes tous les mois)

Inscrivez ici les sources de dépense	Qui ?	Inscrivez le montant	Inscrivez u
Loyer + Charge		750	
Taxe d'habitation		100	
Electricité + Chauffage + Eau Chaude		140	
Eau		30	
Impôts sur le revenu Personne 1		150	
Abonnement musique		9,9	
Frais de garde		0	
Assurance habitation		59	
Assurance voiture		75	
Forfait téléphone port.		19	
Essence		75	
Internet		45	
Cantine ou repas du midi		200	
Carte de transport (50% employeur)		35	
Nourriture		300	
Carte de cinéma		35	
Abonnements divers (chaînes T.V., magasines, ...)		50	

Music subscription:

1.   Do you use your subscription? Yes, No, Very little, Sometimes, From time to time....

2.   How many times a day/month? Every day, once a week, once a month, I can't even say it....

3.   Could you do without it or use a free service with ads? Why not, I never thought about it....

It is important to always have a service adapted to your real needs. We pay far too many useless or unsuitable subscriptions. So what are you going to do?

The mobile phone package:

Don't worry, I'm not going to ask you to ask yourself the same questions as before. In our time, the mobile phone has become such an essential object that it is very difficult to get rid of it.

As I write these lines, there are dozens of packages to adapt to your needs. I have selected, below, some examples far from the good old package at 19.90€/month:

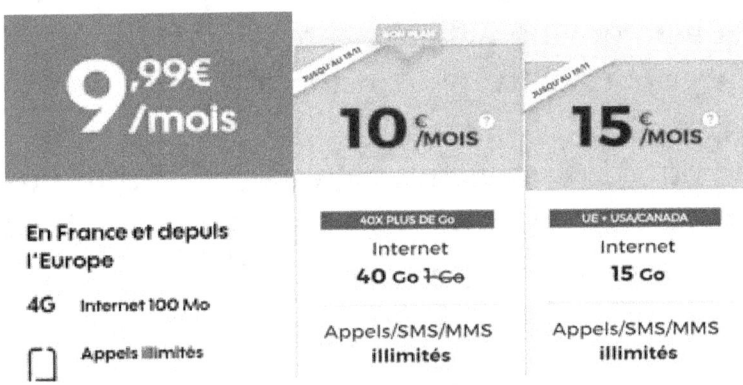

You can also count on the famous 2€/month package. I grant you far from the same advantages as the €19.90 offer but which can still do the trick for a certain type of consumer.

Let's take a personal example: My Grandmother very quickly switched to the fixed price of 2€/month, she who was still paying for rechargeable cards at the time; I can tell you that this changed her life and made her save a lot of money.

It is up to you to assess your use and adapt it to your real needs. Especially since today it is extremely simple and most packages are without commitment.

With a simple click on the internet you can change operators and unsubscribe automatically, it is your new operator who will take care of everything (number portability, line unsubscription).

And even if you still have a package that commits you for a period of more than 12 months, which is increasingly rare since it is now prohibited, you can enforce the Chatel law.

Did you say the Chatel law? What the hell is that? If you have a mobile plan with a commitment of more than 12 months, and well from the end of the twelfth month, you will be able to unsubscribe from your plan at a more advantageous rate. Indeed, you will "simply" have to pay 25% of the amount of your remaining monthly payments until the end of the contract.

To do this, simply write a termination letter (sample letter below) or simply subscribe to another operator who will take care of everything. Your former operator will then charge you 25% of the remaining amount due, one point is all!

To understand this, I suggest you take an example -

You are the proud owner of an extraordinary phoner package at 50€ per month all-inclusive (internet, S.M.S., M.M.S. unlimited) and are committed for 24 months (because you bought with a state-of-the-art phone). After 12 months of engagement, you decide to cancel your phone package and send a registered letter mentioning the Chatel law. Your operator will be obliged to terminate your contract. However, he will invoice you 25% of the remaining sums due: 12 remaining monthly payments x 50€/month x 25% = 150€ instead of 600€ if you had stayed until the end of the commitment period. **Interesting, isn't it?**

Note that, if you wish to take back a telephone package from another operator, you will not even have to write a registered letter, just register and your new operator will take care of all the administrative procedures (number portability, termination...).

To help you get started, I offer you a sample termination letter for your gym for example (to be adapted according to your needs). You remember, this room in which more than 6 out of 10 people stopped in the first 6 months after their registration (Source: UFC Que-choisir) and of course continued to pay....

It's up to you....

Model letter - Fill in the highlighted fields with your information:

Prénom Nom
Mon adresse,
Mon code postal – Ma Ville

Nom de ma salle de sport
Adresse de ma salle de sport
Code postal de ma salle – Ville de ma salle

Objet : Résiliation de mon abonnement dans votre salle de sport.

Madame, Monsieur,

Membre de votre club de sport et titulaire d'une carte de membre (N°xxxxxxxxx), je vous informe de ma volonté de résilier mon contrat d'abonnement.

En effet, la clause relative à la résiliation me donne la faculté d'interrompre mon contrat. Par conséquent, mon abonnement prendra fin au xx/xx/xxxx,

Je vous saurai donc gré de bien vouloir cesser tout prélèvement sur mon compte à compter de cette date.

Avec mes remerciements, veuillez accepter, Madame, Monsieur, l'expression de ma considération distinguée.

Ma signature

Prénom Nom

The model letters are, in most cases, in this format. Feel free to modify them according to the service to be terminated.

Come on, before you continue reading this guide, stop and start terminating a subscription. Choose one and do it.
Come on, don't think you'll do it later, do it really, stop reading and go ahead.

Is it done? So? It wasn't that complicated? To consume without moderation for anything that seems useless, or unbearable to you: -)

Remember that "it is the small streams that make the big rivers (Ovide)" >>> All these savings put together will allow you to save significant sums.

But for the less patient and those who like "big" numbers, know that there is an even more effective way to make very, very big savings.

But then what are these means that require little effort and can make you earn a lot of money?

According to the Yougov Institute, in 2018, active French people spend an average of €10 per day on lunch. That is a total amount of about 220€ per month. A figure that suggests potential savings.

Imagine, if you divided this expense by a quarter you would save nearly €660 every year and if you divided it by half, you could save €1320 every year. But you're going to tell me: "you have to eat well", and you're absolutely right and to eat at a lower cost, there's a simple method, be careful, are you ready?

All you have to do is bring your lunchbox to work and it will cost you almost nothing. It is not a matter of doing it every day, but doing it 2 to 3 times a week would significantly reduce costs.

Let's take an example -

Christine has read this guide and has decided to prepare her lunch 3 times a week.
Before she spent, like most French people, 50€ per week on lunch breaks (a French person spends an average of 10€ per day on lunch), which made a total annual expenditure of 2300€ (50€ per week x 46 weeks worked).
Today she spends only 20€ per week or 920€ per year for a total saving of 1380€ per year or 115€ per month. **Isn't that great? And so easy**....

You will tell me: "Yes, it's easy but your calculation is not complete, you have to take into account the money spent to make your own tusk. "And you are absolutely right, I haven't found any official figures, but you can be sure that the savings will remain well over 1000€ per year. **Take the test!**

There is another equally simple way to save money. Of course you have to have the opportunity, but if you do, then take the train instead of the car.
The expenses related to the use of a vehicle are considerable, in addition to petrol, annual repairs, consumables (windscreen wipers, windscreen washers, oil...), maintenance costs, etc... etc... etc..
Depending on the region, your vehicle costs you a fortune, I invite you to consult the map below which, I hope, will make you think twice before you take your car:

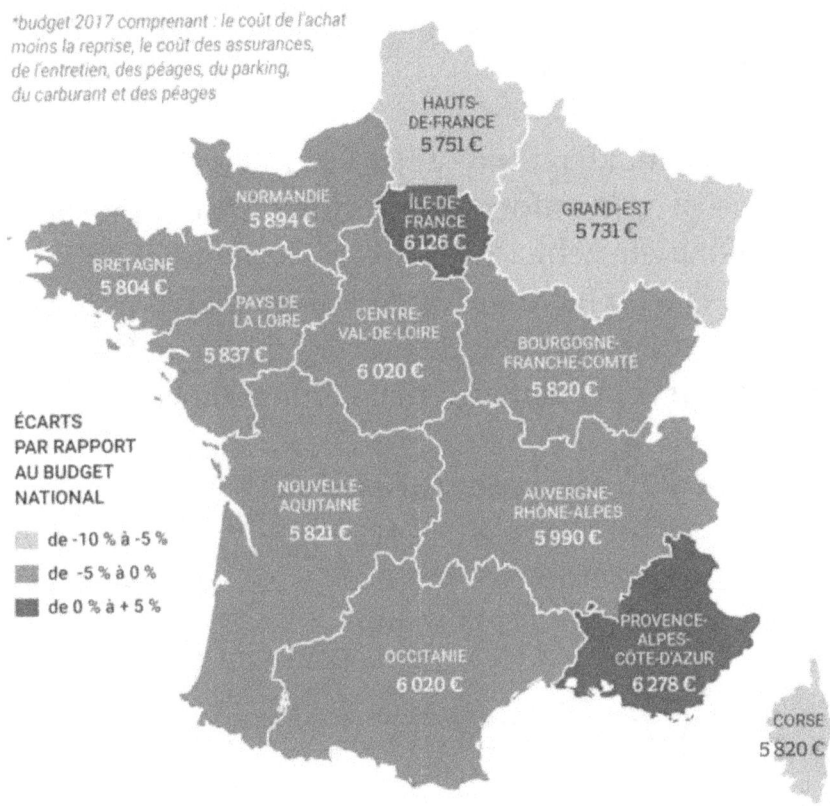

BUDGET AUTOMOBILE MOYEN* PAR RÉGION POUR UN VÉHICULE ESSENCE

budget 2017 comprenant : le coût de l'achat moins la reprise, le coût des assurances, de l'entretien, des péages, du parking, du carburant et des péages

HAUTS-DE-FRANCE
5 751 €

NORMANDIE
5 894 €

ÎLE-DE-FRANCE
6 126 €

GRAND-EST
5 731 €

BRETAGNE
5 804 €

PAYS DE LA LOIRE
5 837 €

CENTRE-VAL-DE-LOIRE
6 020 €

BOURGOGNE-FRANCHE-COMTÉ
5 820 €

NOUVELLE-AQUITAINE
5 821 €

AUVERGNE-RHÔNE-ALPES
5 990 €

PROVENCE-ALPES-CÔTE-D'AZUR
6 278 €

OCCITANIE
6 020 €

CORSE
5 820 €

ÉCARTS PAR RAPPORT AU BUDGET NATIONAL

- de -10 % à -5 %
- de -5 % à 0 %
- de 0 % à + 5 %

Source : Le Budget de l'Automobiliste© 22 / ACA Mars 2018

To give you a concrete example, if you live in the Paris region, your vehicle will cost you about 500 euros per month all inclusive (insurance, garage, maintenance, fuel, toll...).

While a Navigo all-zone pass costs only 770 euros a year. Either an economy total of 5230 euros per year (car = 500 euros per month x 12 months = 6000 euros - navigo pass = 770 euros). **So convinced?**

Please don't make me say what I didn't write, I know that some people unfortunately don't have a choice but to take their vehicle; this example is only for individuals who have the opportunity to make that choice but still prefer the comfort of their car. See how much it costs you and make your choice freely.

Let's go back to our practical case -

With all the examples we have just seen, it is easy to modify or even delete some items:

Dépenses (ce sont les montants qui sont débités de vos comptes tous les mois)

Incrivez ici les sources de dépense	Qui ?	Inscrivez le montant	Inscrivez u
Loyer + Charge		750	
Taxe d'habitation		100	
Electricité + Chauffage + Eau Chaude		140	
Eau		30	
Impôts sur le revenu Personne 1		150	
Abonnement musique		~~9,9~~	
Frais de garde		0	
Assurance habitation		59	
Assurance voiture		75	
Forfait téléphone port.		~~19~~ 9,90€	
Essence		75	
Internet		~~45~~ 7,99€	
Cantine ou repas du midi		~~200~~ 150€	
Carte de transport (50% employeur)		35	
Nourriture		300 250€	
Carte de cinéma		~~35~~	
Abonnements divers (chaînes T.V., magasines, ...)		~~50~~ 25€	

In our example above, we deleted the "Music" expense and opted to use a third-party application even if there were ads.

After going to mobile package comparators, we opted for a cheaper package, we also cut our various subscriptions by two and took the challenge of gradually reducing our expenses in canteen and daily food.

You will notice that I did not deliberately push the figures to the extreme, indeed, I could have reduced the canteen expenses to 0.00€ by applying the example explained above of Christine who prepares her meal. But my objective is to make you understand that even with a minimum of effort, it is possible to afford its famous 13th month.

Believe me, all these savings are real and easy to implement. In addition, I guarantee that you will see the benefits from the first month. That is why they are called immediate savings.

Before moving on to the next chapter and taking stock of what we have already saved, here are two easy ways to save money:

The first is the following, **NEGOTIATE**, indeed, do not hesitate to renegotiate your contracts every year. What are you risking? At worst a refusal? And then at least you've tried it and if it works, it can pay you a lot.

Let's take a personal example. It didn't escape your attention that in the table above, I had reduced my internet package to 7.99€ per month:

Essence	15
Internet	-45- 7,99€
Continuum	200 15.00

You will tell me that this package does not exist on the market. And I would say that you are absolutely right. **But...** But then why such a price and what is behind it? A big scam on my part, a lie or what do I know, a mistake? Well no, that's the price I pay, theproof in pictures:

27/09/2018
7,99€   ✓ Payé le 05/10 ›

27/08/2018
7,99€   ✓ Payé le 04/09 ›

27/07/2018
7,99€   ✓ Payé le 03/08 ›

You're going to tell me that this is a promotional offer and that it will stop as fast as it started.

Well, no, it's just a good example of the A.B.C. of savings (seen in Chapter 6) and a negotiation that cost me a single phone call to the termination service of the operator in question.

So what did I actually do?

1.   I applied the A.B.C. method of savings and more particularly the "A", is it adapted to my needs. Indeed, I don't watch much television or only DTT channels. For series and movies I have a "Apple T.V." type box,

2.   So I asked myself the question of the usefulness of a TV box with my internet subscription and hastened to contact customer service. Who answered me that they had nothing to offer, and that the triple play offer (internet, TV, telephone) was the only possible offer.

3.   I therefore contacted the termination department asking them to close my line by mentioning the Chatel law (refer to chapter 7). They immediately asked me why I wanted to cancel, so I explained to them that my package was not adapted to my needs and that I was going to one of their competitors.

4.   They offered me a double play offer (internet, phone) at 7.99€ per month that I accepted.

In all, it cost me two calls and a little bit of my time. On a classic package at 19.90€ per month, this still saves 11.91€ per month or 142.92€ per year. Not bad for something that didn't cost me anything in time, right? And it has been going on for 3 years.... :-)

My second example is just as simple to set up and will not require any effort on your part.

Remember in *Chapter 6 - The A.B.C.* of Savings, we talked about sports halls, as a reminder: more than 6 out of 10 people stopped in the first 6 months after their registration (Source U.F.C. Que-Choisir). And of course they continued to pay... It is very easy today to play sports for free and in a much more motivating way than having to go out in the morning early before work, between noon and two or in the evening after work.

Think of the hundreds of YouTube channels that allow you to get moving for free without leaving your home and for €0.00. If you need to escape and leave your home, nothing could be easier, go running in town or in the forest, it's a good way to evacuate at a lower cost.

You can even add to this exercises of muscular strengthening that you can find countless and free on the internet.

You're not convinced? Let's do a very simple calculation: A gym costs an average of 29.90€ per month. You multiply this number by 12 months, which makes a total of about 360€ per year that you could save. Easy, isn't it? So are you going enough at the gym? If the answer is no then terminate there (go to the *Model Letter* section in Chapter 7).

SUMMARY -

✓ Cancel your unnecessary subscriptions,

✓ There are no small economies,

✓ Choose homemade meals instead of your canteen or traditional lunch sandwich,

✓ **If you can**, abandon your vehicle,

✓ Renegotiate your contracts over and over again.

Chapter N° 8 - Immediate savings, time for assessment

All this for what? It's time to take stock and see how much you've really saved with our case study:

Dépenses (ce sont les montants qui sont débités de vos comptes tous les mois)

Incrivez ici les sources de dépense	Qui ?	Inscrivez le montant	Inscrivez u
Loyer + Charge		750	
Taxe d'habitation		100	
Electricité + Chauffage + Eau Chaude		140	
Eau		30	
Impôts sur le revenu Personne 1		150	
Abonnement musique		~~9,9~~	
Frais de garde		0	
Assurance habitation		59	
Assurance voiture		75	
Forfait téléphone port.		~~19~~ 9,90€	
Essence		75	
Internet		~~45~~ 7,99€	
Cantine ou repas du midi		~~200~~ 150€	
Carte de transport (50% employeur)		35	
Nourriture		300 250€	
Carte de cinéma		~~35~~	
Abonnements divers (chaînes T.V., magasines, ...)		~~50~~ 25€	

- ✓ Music subscription, 9€ less,
- ✓ Telephone package, €9.10 less,
- ✓ Internet subscription €37.01 less,
- ✓ Canteen or lunch, 50€ less,
- ✓ Food, 50€ less,
- ✓ Movie card, 35€ less,
- ✓ Various subscriptions, 25€ less.

These sums may seem trivial to you, but put together they constitute a real economy. That is why people too often do not even pay attention to it, and yet the gain is significant. See for yourself, you have saved a total of: 216.01€ per month for a total of 2592.12€ per year.

BRAVO to you! You can be proud of yourself!

Now, if we look at the figures from our concrete case, we were in deficit every month from:

= - 172,9 €

Chaque mois vous dépensez plus que ce que vous gagnez il faut donc rééquilibrer vos comptes

Today and with the savings made, we are beneficiaries of: 216.01€ - 172.9€ = 43.11€ per month, representing a savings opportunity of 517.32€ per year.

All this is very positive, but we are still a long way from our 13th month, you will tell me.

Be patient, I invite you to read the next chapter to talk about the possible savings that we don't necessarily think about but that will certainly lead you to your long-awaited 13th month.

Chapter N°.9 - Possible savings

We saw in the previous chapter a direct and very easy way to save money.

In this new chapter, we will discuss the same method but on slightly different cases. Possible savings, which are not always considered because they are too often perceived as complicated to implement.

I reassure you and you will see through examples and the next practical case that it is not really that complicated and that you can save a lot of money.

These are savings that require some research on the Internet. When I talk about research, I am not talking about archaeological research that will take you a long time, no, I am talking about simple research on comparators who have already done all or almost all the work for you.
Remember in chapter 6 of the comparators of the U.F.C. site Que-choisir (https://www.quechoisir.org/). I have no action in them, but I really advise them because they have the advantage of being totally neutral in the sense that there are no partnerships or trade agreements.

Let's take up our concrete case -

Dépenses (ce sont les montants qui sont débités de vos comptes tous les mois)

Incrivez ici les sources de dépense	Qui ?	Inscrivez le montant		Inscrivez u
Loyer + Charge			750	700€
Taxe d'habitation			100	
Electricité + Chauffage + Eau Chaude			140	130€
Eau			30	
Impôts sur le revenu Personne 1			150	
Abonnement musique			9,9	
Frais de garde			0	
Assurance habitation			59	30€
Assurance voiture			75	35€
Forfait téléphone port.			19	
Essence			75	
Internet			45	
Cantine ou repas du midi			200	
Carte de transport (50% employeur)			35	
Nourriture			300	
Carte de cinéma			35	
Abonnements divers (chaînes T.V., magasines, ...)			50	

Your rent is probably one of the most important costs of your expenses, but have you asked yourself the question: "Is it suitable for my needs? ». Indeed, you could very well live in an apartment with 3 bedrooms, while your children have left or live in very expensive cities like Versailles just to have a nice business card....

I'm not saying that everyone is, and you need a minimum of comfort, I'll give you that. But many people live in housing or in a city that is not adapted to their needs and/or budget, so that they end up paying high rents when they would only have to take up a smaller or more distant area.

A friend of mine is a perfect example. She works in the Yvelines in a ready-to-wear store and lives in a city where rents are relatively high, her rent is 790€ per month. In addition, her home is about 15 kilometres from her workplace and she goes there by car.

One weekend, while we were discussing the budget, she told me she was having trouble getting by and finishing her month. In all friendship, I then advised her to take a more suitable accommodation in the city where she works for example; count about 590€ per month for the same surface area, but she replied that she did not want to because she was too used to her comfort and daily routine, despite my arguments:

1.   A comfort because she could walk to work,
2.   A saving on the cost of his rent,
3.   A saving on the costs related to his vehicle.

Not insignificant savings since estimated, only for the rent at 200€ per month, or 2400€ per year, and I am not even talking about the costs related to his vehicle (gasoline, obsolescence,...).

Nothing was done, she never wanted to move, evoking a whole bunch of arguments without any real basis. I'll call it "laziness": -x

Go figure... I didn't want to get angry and our discussion ended there. And the best part of it all is that today she continues to talk to me about her financial difficulties at the end of the month (in the order of a few hundred euros...).

A second and most important position to review every year is your insurance and loans of all kinds.

And here again, I invite you to consult the comparators of car, electricity, gas and other insurance... You will save hundreds of extra euros every year.

I know what you're telling yourself: "it's tedious, it's long, it's restrictive...", but believe me, not at all, especially since most companies do everything or almost everything for you.

So don't wait any longer, go ahead and save money!

In what I call the savings possible, bank loans and especially real estate loans remain our pet peeve in the sense that we always believe that changing banks is complicated. But nay, it's as simple as changing your mobile phone plan.

You do not believe me ? And the service of support to the banking mobility it speaks to you? Are you curious?

So read on:

The bank mobility support service is a measure of the law for growth, activity and equal economic opportunities, known as the Macron law. It came into effect on February 6, 2017, and now it is the destination bank, which you have chosen, to perform for you **all the steps** related to a change of account. Nice no?

You're going to say yes it's great but how to find a new loan, how to know that it's more advantageous, how to subscribe to it, it's a long, boring and often head-on process. And you're absolutely right. I myself, who are always looking to reduce my expenses, admit that this position rejects me, or rather discourages me...

What if I told you that there is a simple and inexpensive solution that allows you, without leaving your home, to take all these steps:

- ✓ Find a bank loan,
- ✓ Find the best possible rate,
- ✓ Take the administrative steps with the banks and meet with your banker only to sign the final document,

This solution is called...**A Broker**.

Personally, I went through a broker for all my real estate purchases and each time I was satisfied.

He takes care of everything but then absolutely everything. You correspond with him by e-mail, scan documents for him and that's it! The day you see him, it will be to sign the final loan agreement. Comfortable, isn't it?

But how much does it cost? Between 600€ and 1500€ per service but considering what it will save you, it is really worth it.

Let's take a very simple example at understand:

Your current loan -

Borrowed amount: 200,000€,
Duration: 20 years,
Rate excluding insurance: 5.05%,
Loan insurance: 0.36%,
Outstanding amount to be repaid: 173735€,
Remaining repayment period: 191 months,
Monthly payment: 1325 €per month.

✓ This means a total credit cost of 253075€.

Loan proposed by the Broker -

Amount to be borrowed: €182,353 (yes, it is higher than the amount still to be repaid because it includes the penalties for credit repurchase and other related costs),
Remaining repayment period: 191 months,
Rate excluding insurance: 2.95%,
Loan insurance: 0.27%,
Monthly payment: €1197 per month.

✓ This means a total credit cost of €228,722.

This will save you a total of: 253075 – 228722 = **24353€.**

So? It's not much compared to the ~1000€ spent at a broker, is it?

Now that you have all the balls in hand, it's up to you!

SUMMARY -

- ✓ Change accommodation or take adapted accommodation,

- ✓ Compete and change contracts with the Macron law,

- ✓ Use the services of professionals such as brokers, you will save time and money (feel free to contact me from my website: **https://jd-paris.fr** if you want to be referred to a good broker)

Chapter N° 10 - Possible savings, time for assessment

It's time to do the math and see how much you've really saved with our case study:

Dépenses (ce sont les montants qui sont débités de vos comptes tous les mois)

Incrivez ici les sources de dépense	Qui ?	Inscrivez le montant		Inscrivez u
Loyer + Charge			750	700€
Taxe d'habitation			100	
Electricité + Chauffage + Eau Chaude			140	130€
Eau			30	
Impôts sur le revenu Personne 1			150	
Abonnement musique			9,9	
Frais de garde			0	
Assurance habitation			59	30€
Assurance voiture			75	35€
Forfait téléphone port.			19	
Essence			75	
Internet			45	
Cantine ou repas du midi			200	
Carte de transport (50% employeur)			35	
Nourriture			300	
Carte de cinéma			35	
Abonnements divers (chaînes T.V., magasines, ...)			50	

✓ Rent, 50€ less,
✓ Electricity, water..., 10€ less,
✓ Various insurances, 69€ less.

That is a total saving of: 129€ per month for a total of 1548€ each year.

CONGRATULATION

Now remember, in Chapter 8 we had a net profit of €43.11 per month, or a savings opportunity of €517.32 per year. Not enough to afford a 13th month.

But with the possible savings we have just made, you will go from 43.11€ per month to 172.11€ per month (43.11€ + 129€) or 2065.32€ per year.

There you go! There you go! Your long-awaited 13th month is finally possible and will amount to **2065.32€.** The most difficult thing will be to decide what you will do with it.

Chapter N° 11 - Conclusion

We are at the end of this guide and we have seen through the various examples and our practical case what could be achieved in terms of savings. All the examples I have shown you are extremely easy to set up and for an amazing result. Isn't that right? Did you think that such small end-to-end savings could make you that much money?

Indeed, not only have you managed to fill your deficit by:

= - 172,9 €

Chaque mois vous dépensez plus que ce que vous gagnez il faut donc rééquilibrer vos comptes

But you have also increased your purchasing power by more than 2000 euros per year.

Imagine now, that if tomorrow you decide to go even further by reselling your vehicle and favouring the train instead, removing all the superfluous, making your own lunch, etc... you could claim thousands of euros in savings every year. And that's exactly what my wife and I did, nothing more. I invite you to consult the blog below:
http://vie-de-maman.net/

Remember:

✓ Make your meals at home, 1320€ less,
✓ Take the train instead of your car, 5230€ less,
✓ Reduce your Internet package, €142.92 less,
✓ Cancel your gym membership and play sports at home, €358.80 less,
✓ ...

This means a possible saving of €587.64 per month or €7051.72 per year. **Considerable, isn't it?**

Now that you know all this and have all the keys to success, your biggest challenge will not be to find ways to fill your overdraft but rather to find out how to use your money:-)

We are coming to the end of this guide, which I hope will have helped you to realize how much savings can be easily achieved. To be convinced, I really invite you to take action, don't be passive or sceptical, be curious to try it and I guarantee you won't regret it.

For those who still think it's too tedious, difficult, that it can't be that simple otherwise everyone would do it, I invite you to contact me from my website: **https://jd-paris.fr** and choose the following formula:

PERSONNALISÉ

Then we can do the exercise together. I hope it will definitely erase your last doubts and lead you to your 13th month and much more....

BONUS - Ideas for better budget management

"For lots of good advice, I strongly encourage you to visit the website: "**http://vie-de-maman.net/**".

As a reminder, 85% of French people have not received any budgetary and financial education, whether at school, university, in their company or in a specialised institute (IFOP 2016 survey).
By providing the keys to understanding how the economy works and enabling people to make informed financial decisions, financial education also contributes to strengthening financial stability and economic growth.

Established in 2016 on the basis of the high-level principles developed by the OECD and adopted by the G20, the financial education strategy aims to provide everyone with the economic, budgetary and financial basis to make informed financial decisions throughout their lives.

The field of financial education is vast, covering both budgetary education (personal or family budget), learning banking tools (daily banking, savings, insurance), as well as understanding economic concepts (functioning and financing of the economy) and public policies (extract from the website **http://economie.gouv.fr**).

Throughout this reading, we have been interested in personal and family budget education and I invite you to read these few BONUS tips to help you in your quest to spend ever better:

Monthlyize yourself -

It is much easier to follow a budget when your expenses are monthly. This avoids, for example, forgetting at the end of the year the different property taxes, housing taxes, income taxes, etc. So spread your various expenses over time.

Sell anything you don't need –

There are dozens of websites or mobile applications that can sell almost anything. Le bon coin and Ebay allow you to put online and sell all your items for free without having to wait for a flea market. It is very easy to put an ad online and make money.
 Then go for it!

Prefer the opportunity -

As seen above, you can easily sell and buy used products on the internet. Whether it's for a birthday, a celebration or even Christmas, don't be ashamed and buy second-hand gifts.

According to the OpinionWay survey, one in two French people has already resold a Christmas gift or is considering doing so. A figure that rises to 63% for 18-34 year olds, or more than 6 out of 10 French people.

The market has become more democratic and it is becoming easier and easier to buy second-hand toys on the web and therefore cheaper. These gifts, known as "second-hand" gifts, are much more profitable than sales in the sense that products are generally sold 30% to 60% cheaper than the new price. Interesting, isn't it?

So why not you? Personally, after a long hesitation, I passed the milestone.

What decided me was not the financial aspect at first but rather the fact that I have two young boys and two beautiful nieces who at Christmas or their birthdays prefer to play with the boxes rather than the toy itself. And even when these little kids deign to be interested in the toy, it never lasts very long.

So I decided to go on the internet and in different toy stores to buy my gifts (Christmas, birthday, holidays, etc....). Imagine that beyond saving hundreds of euros, I realized that the majority of toys were almost new, some were still in their original packaging and sold 10 times cheaper than in stores.

I give you an example that impressed me -

"A radio car ordered Mickey - Disney - First age" sold for about thirty euros in stores and paid only two euros in an impeccable condition!

Thousands of objects like this exist so go ahead and it's good for the planet:-)

Prefer cash payment to credit card -

We have seen in the previous chapters that it is possible to make significant savings, particularly on the food budget, an item of expenditure that is also very important for families. To make sure you don't exceed a budget allocated to an expense item, take out cash and don't touch your credit card.

Having cash allocated to a position will allow you to:

✓ Be aware of what you are spending,
✓ Be careful not to overspend,
✓ To realize what you have left,
✓ Not to exceed your budget.

Feel free to do it now!

Finally and to conclude this practical guide, I invite you to review your accounts regularly. Ideally, each time an expense is changed, but once every three months may be sufficient. What is important is that you be aware that managing your budget is essential and the rest will follow.

Congratulations to you for having reached the end of this reading, now you have all the balls to perfectly manage your expenses and save money.

I will soon write another guide on financial independence or how to create assets and limit liabilities. What is it? What is it? Active? Liabilities? What are these swear words?

Don't worry, nothing very complicated and it will allow you to turn all your expenses, everything that costs you money today into income. Yes, you read well in income! Are you skeptical? How much does your car cost you per month? 500€? How about renting it for €525 a month? How? How? Well, there are sites and applications for that, **and it works**!

So keep following us on **https://jd-paris.fr** and good luck with your financial independence.

"Make your life a dream, and a dream a reality. " (Antoine de Saint-Exupéry)

BONUS - A 100% practical case study

.:. Many of you have asked me that:
>>> Download a concrete and 100% practical
example available at the following address:
https://jd-paris.fr/ressources/Cas_pratique.7z

www.ingramcontent.com/pod-product-compliance
Lightning Source LLC
Chambersburg PA
CBHW070607220526
45467CB00003B/1334